HUMAN BODY

Richard Walker

Papilla

A Golden Photo Guide from St. Martin's Press

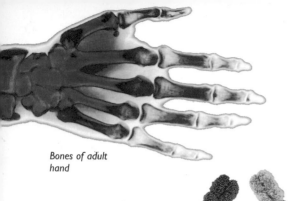
Bones of adult hand

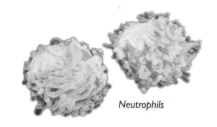
Neutrophils

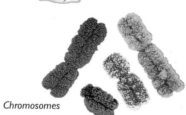
Chromosomes

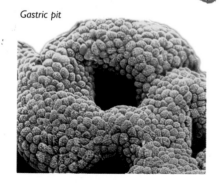
Gastric pit

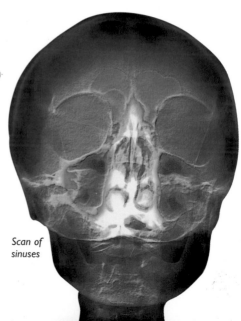
Scan of sinuses

HUMAN BODY

A Golden Photo Guide from St. Martin's Press

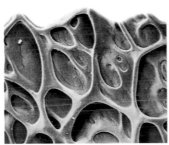

*Gall bladder
lining*

St. Martin's Press
New York
Manufactured in China

Produced by
Elm Grove Books Limited
Series Editor Susie Elwes
Text Editor Angela Wilkes
Art Director Susi Martin
Illustration John Woodcock
Computer Illustration
Chris Taylor
Index Hilary Bird
Original Edition © 2000
Image Quest Limited
This edition © 2001
Elm Grove Books Limited

**St. Martin's Press
175 Fifth Avenue
New York N.Y. 10010.
www.stmartins.com**

A CIP catalogue record for this
book is available from the Library
of Congress

ISBN 1-58238-177-1

Text and Photographs in this book
previously published in
Eyewitness 3D Human Body

This edition published 2001

ACKNOWLEDGMENTS
Roger Chinn: 11c, 13c, 17c; **Lupe Cunha**: 28l; **Dorling Kindersley**: 18, 21t, 23, 32r, 35bl; **A.B. Dowsett**:5c,
39c; **Andrew Forge**: 26br, 27c, 31c; **David McCarthy**: 6b, 9c, 15c, 23c, 29c, 35c, 37c, 41c, 43c, 45c, 49c, 30br;
Medical Illustrative Group:25c, 47c; **Ray Moss** 11, 19t, 27, 34bl 51c;**Pictor** 31br; **Chris Priest**:: 19c, 21c, 41t;
Science Photo Library: 4, 5, 5, 5, 5, 6t, 7br, 8, 8, 9, 9, 10l,11br, 12, 12, 13, 13, 14, 14, 15, 15, 16, 17, 17, 19br, 20,
21b, 22, 22, 23br, 24tl, 25br, 26tl, 27br, 28br, 29, 29, 30bl, 31bl, 33, 33, 33, 34tl, 35cl, 36, 36, 37, 37, 37, 38tl, 38bc,
39, 39, 40, 40, 40, 41br, 42br, 43, 43, 44, 44, 45, 5, 46, 46, 47, 47, 48, 48, 49, 49, 50, 50, 51, 51, 52, 52, 53, 53, 53;
Tony Stone: 4b, 24b, 27tr, 38br, 42tl; **Wim van Egmond**: 33; **Wellcome Trust Medical Photographic
Library**: 7l, 10lb, 25 lb, 26bl

The publishers would like to thank
Chelsea & Westminster Hospital, London
St George's Hospital, London
The Maudsley Hospital, London

CONTENTS

Podocyte

Fungiform papilla

THE BODY

The body is made of trillions of microscopic living units called cells. There are many different types of cell, each with its own function. Cells of the same type form tissues and tissues work together to form organs, such as the heart. Related organs are linked in a system, such as the digestive system. Together all the systems make up the body.

A model of DNA shows it is like a twisted ladder, with two linked strands that spiral around each other.

BODY CODE

DNA – deoxyribonucleic acid – is a complex substance inside the nucleus of every cell in your body. It is packed into threadlike structures called chromosomes. DNA stores all the information needed to run each cell, and to make a complete human being – you. It can also make an exact copy of itself, so that when cells divide each new cell has exactly the same set of instructions.

SMALL DIFFERENCES

As this father and son show, no two humans look exactly the same. Despite their differences, all people, whether male or female, have the same basic body structure. People also follow a similar pattern of life, starting with infancy, then moving on to adulthood.

CELL DIVISION

Your body produces billions of new cells each day. It does this by a process called cell division. Cell division is essential for growth, and for replacing old, worn-out cells.

DIFFERENT CELLS

Here are three of the many different types of cell that make up your body. They look different from each other because they have different functions. All cells have the same internal structure.

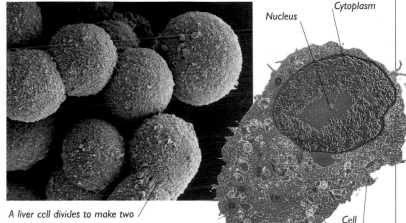

A liver cell divides to make two identical copies of itself.

Nucleus

Cytoplasm

Cell membrane

ALL IN A CELL

The nucleus is the control center of a cell. Chemical reactions that keep the cell alive take place in the cytoplasm. The cell membrane surrounds the cell.

Bone cell

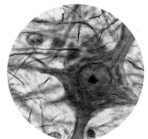

Brain cell

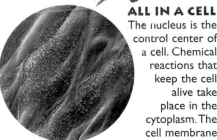

Skin cell

SKIN

Skin is a flexible, waterproof, germ-proof barrier between the inside of the body and the outside world. It is the largest organ in the body. It has sensors to detect touch, pressure, heat, and pain. Skin has two layers. A thick inner layer, the dermis, contains nerve endings and blood vessels. A thin outer layer, the epidermis, is made from tough, protective cells. The epidermis is replaced constantly, day by day, as it is worn away.

FINGERPRINT
A fingerprint is the mark left on an object by the thin film of oily sweat that covers the ridges on your fingertips. Each fingerprint is unique to its owner.

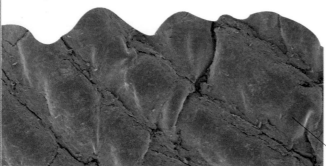

TINY RIDGES
The skin on the undersides of your fingers and toes, the palms of your hands, and the soles of your feet has a surface covered by tiny ridges. These ridges help you to grip things with smooth surfaces.

Microscopic view of the ridges on a thumb. Each ridge is no more than 0.04 inch (1 mm) high.

SOLE SKIN

The skin covering most of your body is about 0.05 inch (1.5 mm) thick. The skin on the sole of your foot is about 0.16 inch (4 mm) thick. Skin is thicker and tougher on your feet because they suffer more wear and tear.

Flakes of skin collect on the sole of a foot as the thick skin wears away.

SWEATY SKIN

Sweat is a salty liquid produced by sweat glands in your skin. When your body is too hot, sweat is released onto the surface of the skin. There it evaporates and draws heat from the body and cools it down.

A sweat pore, the opening of a sweat gland, beside a drop of sweat it has released.

MELANIN

This section through skin shows a layer of brown melanin. Melanin, produced by the epidermis, colors the skin and protects it from harmful ultraviolet rays in sunlight.

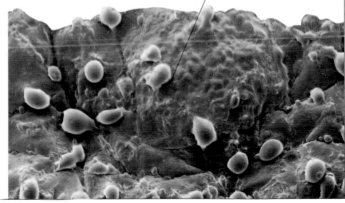

HAIR AND NAILS

Hair and nails grow from the skin. Fine hairs cover most of your body, and grow from deep pits in the skin called hair follicles. Coarser hair grows thickly on the head and eyebrows. All adults grow some coarse body hair. Most men shave the coarse hair on their faces every day. Nails protect the tips of fingers and toes and help the fingers to grip objects. Hair and nails are made of dead cells, so it does not hurt when either are cut.

The end of the hair shaft is split into separate strands.

SPLIT ENDS

If your hair is not cut regularly, is lacking in natural oils, or treated with chemical bleaches and dyes, the ends of the hairs may shatter. This condition, called split ends, makes hairs stick together and look matted.

NAIL SURFACE

Magnified, the surface of a nail shows layers of dead cells packed with tough keratin. Nails grow from living cells at their base about 0.2 inch (5 mm) each month. As cells grow they die, move forward, and fill with keratin.

Dead nail cells slot tightly together to form a protective surface.

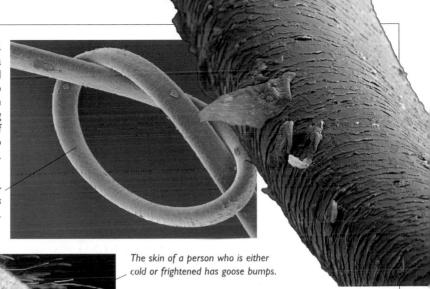

FLEXIBLE HAIR

Hair is made mainly of a tough protein called keratin, the material also found in nails. Keratin in the hair makes it strong and flexible. A strand of hair can easily be tied into a knot without breaking.

This curly hair is oval-shaped. Straight hair is round in shape.

The skin of a person who is either cold or frightened has goose bumps.

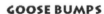

GOOSE BUMPS

When a person gets cold, tiny muscles in their skin pull on hair follicles and make hairs stand upright. This hair makes tiny bumps, called goose bumps or goose pimples, appear on the skin around the hair follicle.

HAIR SCALES

The hair has three different layers. The outer layer is made of overlapping scales, like fish scales, which may flake off. Inside the outer layer is a layer that contains hair color. The central core may be hollow.

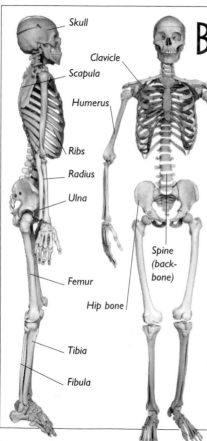

Skull

Clavicle

Scapula

Humerus

Ribs

Radius

Ulna

Spine
(back-
bone)

Femur

Hip bone

Tibia

Fibula

BONY FRAMEWORK

There are 206 bones in the skeleton of an adult human. The skeleton provides a bony framework that supports the body and gives it shape. It also protects delicate internal organs, such as the brain inside the skull, and the heart and lungs inside the rib cage. Muscles attached to bones pull on them to make them move.

THE HUMAN SKELETON

The human skeleton has two main parts. The axial skeleton – skull, spine, and ribs – runs down the center of the body. The appendicular skeleton consists of arm and leg bones, shoulders and hips.

A scan of the spine shows the column of cylindrical bones, called vertebrae, separated by discs of cartilage that make the spine flexible.

Vertebra

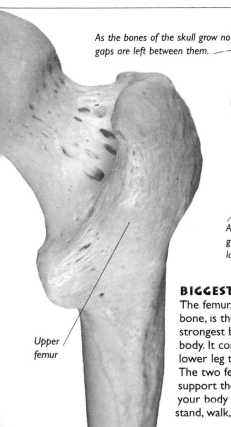

Upper femur

As the bones of the skull grow no gaps are left between them.

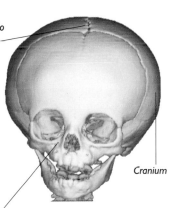

Cranium

A baby's facial bones are small but they grow fast in childhood. As the head grows larger, the face will change.

BABY'S SKULL

This scan of a six-month-old baby's head shows that the cranium, the upper part of the skull that surrounds the brain, is much larger than the skull bones forming the face. The cranium is already half its adult size.

BIGGEST BONES

The femur, or thigh bone, is the longest, strongest bone in the body. It connects the lower leg to the hip. The two femurs support the weight of your body when you stand, walk, or run.

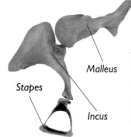

Malleus

Stapes

Incus

SMALLEST BONES

The three ossicles that carry sounds in each ear are your body's smallest bones. Named after their shapes, the ossicles are called the malleus (hammer), incus (anvil), and stapes (stirrup). The smallest bone, the stapes, is only 0.125 inch (3 mm) long.

FLEXIBLE SKELETON

A column of 26 bones called vertebrae make up your spine, or backbone.

Where two or more bones meet, they form a joint. A few joints, such as those between the skull bones, are fixed and don't move. However, most joints allow bones that are connected to each other to move; this gives the skeleton its flexibility. It allows us to walk, run, draw, or play the piano. There are several different types of movable joints, and their movements depend on the shapes of the bone ends inside them.

FLEXIBLE SPINE
The backbone's vertebrae meet at joints that, alone, allow little movement. Together, however, all these joints make the backbone flexible and allow it to bend and twist.

BALL AND SOCKET JOINT
A "ball" at the top of the thigh bone fits into a "socket" in the hip. This flexible joint allows the leg to move in all directions.

FLEXIBLE WRIST

The wrist is made of eight cubelike bones called carpals that link the arm to the hand and fingers. The joints between arm bones and carpals make it possible for the hand to move freely in all directions.

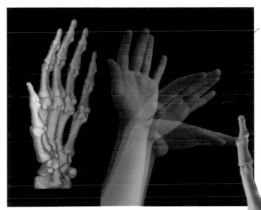

The wrist rotates the hand in a circle.

GLIDING JOINT

Bones that meet in a gliding joint have flat surfaces. This allows the bones to glide slightly over each other. This type of joint is found between your ankle bones.

Gliding joints between the tarsal bones of the foot

WRIST JOINT

A joint where the oval head of one bone fits into the oval cup shape of another is called a condyloid joint. It allows the bones to move up and down and from side to side. This type of joint is found in the wrist.

Radius

Condyloid joint between radius and wrist bones

Ulna

INSIDE BONES

Bone is a living tissue that is as strong as steel but five times lighter. It owes this remarkable property to both its composition and construction. Bone tissue is made of collagen fibers, which give it strength, and calcium and other minerals, which make it extremely hard. Each bone has a hard outer layer of dense, compact bone and an interior of light, spongy bone. The spaces inside bones are filled with jellylike bone marrow.

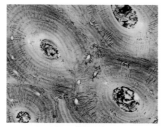

STRONG BONE
Above, a slice of compact bone magnified shows how the bony cylinders, or osteons, are packed lengthwise. This gives compact bone its strength.

BONY CANALS
Inside each osteon, bony tubes, called lamellae, are arranged in layers around a central canal. This canal carries blood vessels to the bone cells, or osteocytes. These bone cells are tucked away in tiny cavities between the lamellae, seen here as dark spots.

Osteocyte cavity

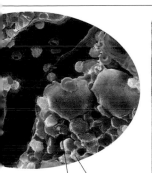

Red blood cells / White blood cells

BONE MARROW

Spongy bone contains a soft tissue called bone marrow. Red bone marrow produces new red blood cells.

In living bones these spaces are filled with red bone marrow. The struts give strong support inside the bone.

INSIDE BONES

Spongy bone has a honeycomb structure of spaces and supporting struts. This type of bone is light and strong although it is not solid.

BONE CELL

A spiderlike bone cell, or osteocyte, sits inside its own tiny cavity in compact bone. Osteocytes maintain the hard bone tissue. They are linked to each other by tiny threads (pale blue) that pass along minute channels in the bone.

GROWTH AND REPAIR

Bones grow and can repair themselves if damaged. Bones start to grow before birth and carry on growing into a person's early twenties. Although bones are strong, sudden extreme pressure can make them fracture, or break. If this happens, bone cells make new bone to repair the fracture. Doctors often use pins or plaster casts to make the broken ends of bones line up together as they heal.

The X-rays show how bones – in this case hand bones – develop from birth to adulthood. In babies and children, part of the skeleton is made of cartilage. Gradually flexible cartilage is replaced by bone (colored pink/blue).

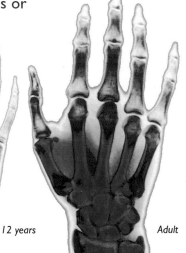

Baby

2 years

12 years

Adult

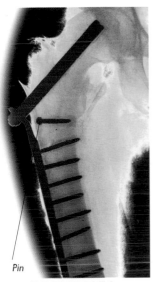

Pin

BROKEN LEG

The head of this femur (thigh bone) has fractured. The fracture has been secured with pins, to fix the head of the bone to its long shaft while the bone repairs itself.

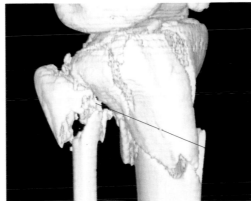

COMPOUND FRACTURE

In a compound fracture, the broken end of a bone pierces the skin. In a simple fracture it does not. The X-ray shows a forearm with compound fracture. Both forearm bones – the radius and ulna – are broken, and the radius is projecting through the skin.

BROKEN KNEE

The long bones of the lower leg – the fibula and tibia – have fractured below the knee cap. To heal they need to be held in place and rested, because the bones in the lower leg support all the weight of the body.

The fibula has snapped where it joins the second leg bone, the tibia.

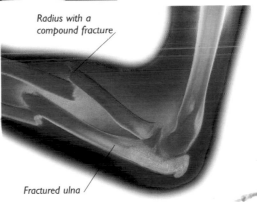

Radius with a compound fracture

Fractured ulna

MUSCLE POWER

Muscles contract (get shorter) to produce movement. The body contains more than 650 skeletal muscles, which make up over 40% of the body's mass. These muscles are attached to the skeleton. When they contract, they pull across joints and move the bones, allowing different types of movements.

When the arm is straight the biceps muscle, fixed to the shoulder and forearm, is long and relaxed.

When a person bends their arm, the triceps starts to relax and lengthen.

The triceps muscle contracts and pulls the forearm bone downward and straightens the arm.

As it gets shorter and fatter, the biceps pulls the forearm up.

The biceps contracts.

The triceps is relaxed.

WORKING MUSCLE

Muscles work by contracting and pulling a bone to make it move, not by pushing it. To move a bone in one direction, upward, requires one muscle, the biceps. To move the arm in the opposite direction, downward, requires a different muscle, the triceps.

The biggest tendon in the body is the Achilles tendon. It links the calf muscle to the heel bone.

This big muscle is called the pectoralis major muscle. It links the chest to the arm.

MUSCLE MAN

The muscles under the skin of this body-builder are easy to see. Bodybuilders train with weights to make their muscles bigger. They also have very little fat under their skin so their muscles stand out clearly.

TENDONS

Muscles are attached to bones by tough cords called tendons. Most of them look like narrow ropes, but some are broad and flat.

Inside myofibril cells, actin and myosin filaments slide over each other and make the muscle fiber shorten.

MUSCLE TISSUE

Muscles are made up of bundles of single threadlike fibers. Muscle fiber is made of cylinders (orange), called myofibrils. Under a microscope these look striped because they contain filaments of proteins called actin and myosin.

BLOOD SUPPLY

This angiogram, a type of X-ray, shows the main arteries supplying blood to the brain. The brain needs a constant supply of blood to provide it with huge amounts of oxygen and energy. The brain forms 2% of your body mass, but it receives about 20% of the body's blood supply.

CONTROL CENTER

Everything you do, from thinking to digesting food, is coordinated by the nervous system. It works by sending rapid messages along nerve cells, called neurons. The brain is the control center of the nervous system. It contains over 100 billion neurons. Each neuron makes contact with thousands of others in a communications network that controls the body's actions.

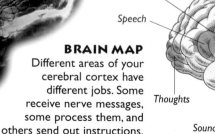

Movement Hearing Touch
Taste Language
Speech

Thoughts

Vision
Sound

BRAIN MAP

Different areas of your cerebral cortex have different jobs. Some receive nerve messages, some process them, and others send out instructions.

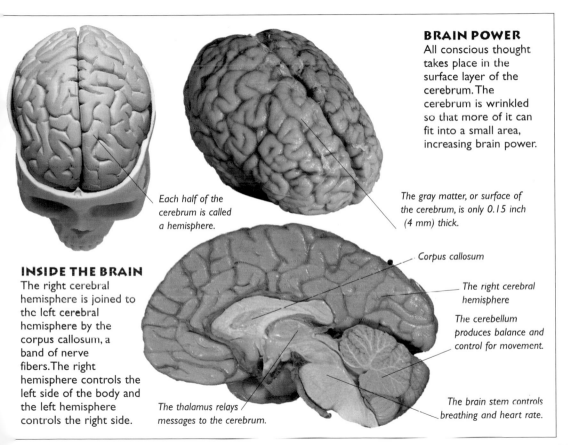

BRAIN POWER
All conscious thought takes place in the surface layer of the cerebrum. The cerebrum is wrinkled so that more of it can fit into a small area, increasing brain power.

Each half of the cerebrum is called a hemisphere.

The gray matter, or surface of the cerebrum, is only 0.15 inch (4 mm) thick.

INSIDE THE BRAIN
The right cerebral hemisphere is joined to the left cerebral hemisphere by the corpus callosum, a band of nerve fibers. The right hemisphere controls the left side of the body and the left hemisphere controls the right side.

Corpus callosum

The right cerebral hemisphere

The cerebellum produces balance and control for movement.

The brain stem controls breathing and heart rate.

The thalamus relays messages to the cerebrum.

NEURONS AND NERVES

Billions of nerve cells, called neurons, make up the nervous system. Neurons carry high-speed electrical signals called nerve impulses. Association neurons are found in the central nervous system or CNS (brain and spinal cord). Sensory neurons carry messages from sensors to the CNS; motor neurons carry messages from the CNS to muscles.

Magnified, a nerve cell appears as a dark blob. These are special nerve cells found in the cerebellum, part of the brain. This part of your brain enables you to balance and move with co-ordination. Nerve impulses pass into these cells through their long fibers.

BRIDGING THE GAP

Where neurons meet, they have to bridge a tiny gap called a synapse. When a nerve impulse arrives at the end of a neuron, the synapse releases chemicals that make the next neuron "fire" and transmit the signal. The same thing happens where a neuron and muscle join.

A nerve impulse passes from a neuron (pink) to a muscle, across a synapse.

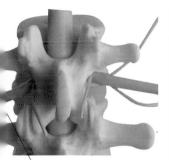

A spinal nerve leaves the spinal cord through a gap between vertebrae.

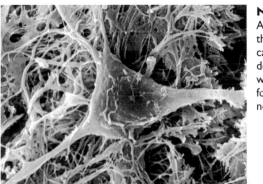

NEURON

A neuron has fine threadlike branches called dendrites. These dendrites make contact with other neurons to form a communications network.

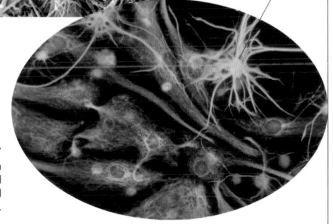

Astrocyte, a type of neuroglia.

COMMUNICATION CORD

The spinal cord is a column of nerve fibers that runs from the brain down a bony channel in the spine. It relays information between the brain and the rest of the body through 31 pairs of spinal nerves. Nerves are bundles of sensory and motor neurons.

CELL SUPPORT

Besides neurons, the nervous system also contains supporting cells called neuroglia. They support neurons and supply them with nutrients.

23

SEEING

It is your senses that enable you to experience the world around you. The sensors for seeing are inside the eyes. Light from the surroundings enters each eye through the cornea at the front of the eyeball and is focused by a lens onto the retina at the back of the eyeball. When hit by light, sensors in the retina send messages to the brain, which interprets them as pictures that are "seen."

Filaments hold the lens in place.

A magnified view of the inner surface of the iris.

IRIS IN CLOSE-UP

The iris is the colored part of the eye. Muscle fibers in the iris contract (shorten) to change the size of the pupil, the hole in the center.

CONTACT LENSES

Contact lenses fit snugly on the clear cornea at the front of the eye. The lenses are used to correct a common problem called myopia, or short-sightedness. To a short-sighted person, distant objects appear blurred. Contact lenses enable people to see everything clearly.

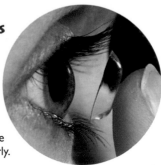

THE RETINA

The retina can be seen by using an ophthalmoscope to look through the pupil into the eye. Nerve fibers from light sensors in the retina unite to form the optic nerve, which carries messages to the brain. Where the optic nerve leaves the eyeball there is a small, paler patch of retina that has no light sensors. This is called the blind spot.

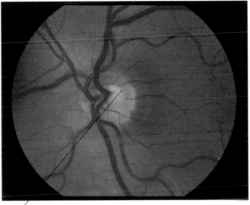

RODS AND CONES

The tiny section of retina below shows some of its 130 million light sensors, called cones and rods. Cones (green-blue) work in bright light and enable a person to see in colour. The more numerous rods (blue) work in dim light, but only provide black and white images.

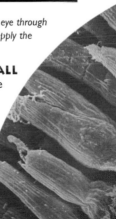

Blood vessels entering and leaving the eye through the blind spot along the optic nerve supply the retina with food and oxygen.

Iris

Pupil narrowed

Pupil widened

PUPILS LARGE AND SMALL

The iris surrounds the pupil, the hole that allows light into the eye. In bright light the iris makes the pupil smaller, to stop too much light entering the eye and damaging the retina. In dim light the pupil widens to let more light into the eye.

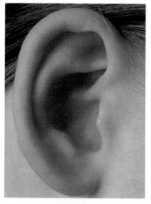

HEARING

Sounds are detected through the ears. Sound waves pass through the air and enter the outer, visible part of the ear. They are then transmitted by the middle ear to the fluid-filled inner ear. Sound detectors in the inner ear send signals to your brain, which interprets them as sounds. Other parts of the inner ear help you to balance.

SHELL-LIKE EAR

The pinna, or ear flap, is made of flexible cartilage covered with skin. The funnel-like curves of the pinna channel sounds into the opening of the auditory canal, which the pinna surrounds.

VIBRATING DRUM

The eardrum is a membrane stretched across the inner end of the ear canal. When sounds enter the ear, the eardrum vibrates. The spiral cochlea in the inner ear is filled with fluid. Sensors inside it pick up sound vibrations passing through the fluid.

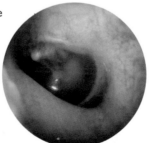

Doctors can see the almost transparent eardrum by inserting an otoscope into the auditory canal.

This view inside the inner ear clearly shows the spiral shape of the cochlea, just 0.25 inch (1 cm) long.

FINE TUNING

Sound detectors inside the cochlea consist of hair cells with sensory hairs attached to a membrane. Sound vibrations passing along the cochlea shake the membrane, which bends the sensory hairs. This makes the hair cells send nerve messages to the brain.

U-shaped row of sensory hairs projecting from a hair cell.

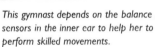

This gymnast depends on the balance sensors in the inner ear to help her to perform skilled movements.

BALANCE

A sense of balance enables people to stand up straight and move without falling over. There are balance sensors in the fluid-filled inner ear. They send messages to the brain as the head changes position, so the brain "knows" about the body's movement and position.

Hairlike cilia protrude from balance sensors in your inner ear. When the fluid moves, the cilia bend and a message is sent to your brain.

TASTE

On the tongue there are about 10,000 taste sensors, called taste buds. The upper surface of the tongue is covered by tiny bumps called papillae. The taste buds are found on or between these bumps. Sensory cells clustered inside each taste bud detect dissolved chemicals in food and drink and send messages to the brain. The four main tastes — sweet, sour, salt, and bitter — are detected by different parts of your tongue.

TASTE CENTER
Round fungiform papillae are shaped like mushrooms. They are scattered over most of the tongue, but especially near its tip. Taste buds are found on the tops and sides of these papillae.

ADDED GRIP

The smallest and most numerous of the bumps on the tongue, called filiform papillae, lack taste buds. These bumps give the tongue a rough surface so that it can grip food during chewing.

BITTER TASTING

Between 8 and 12 large papillae are arranged in an arrow shape at the back of the tongue. The taste buds for bitter tastes are positioned inside the wall surrounding the papilla.

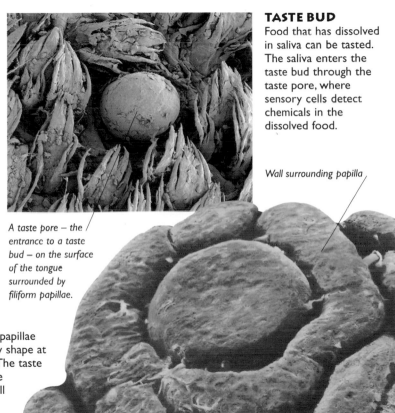

A taste pore – the entrance to a taste bud – on the surface of the tongue surrounded by filiform papillae.

TASTE BUD

Food that has dissolved in saliva can be tasted. The saliva enters the taste bud through the taste pore, where sensory cells detect chemicals in the dissolved food.

Wall surrounding papilla

SINUSES

These air-filled spaces in the skull surround, and are connected to, the nasal cavity. They warm and moisten inhaled air, and drain mucus into the nasal cavity.

SMELL

From freshly baked bread to bad eggs, the sense of smell can detect a huge range of odors. Smell sensors inside the inner part of the nose, called the nasal cavity, detect smells in the air you breathe in. The nose also cleans, warms, and moistens air before it reaches your lungs. Smell and taste together also enable you to experience different flavors.

HAIRY SIEVES

Hairs in your nostrils trap dirt and dust from the air every time you breathe in.

This X-ray of the head shows a large sinus (purple). It is one of several surrounding the nasal cavity.

30

SENSITIVE HAIRS

The lining of the upper nasal cavity is packed with 25 million smell sensors. At the tip of each one are up to 20 tiny cilia, called olfactory hairs. They are coated with watery mucus. When substances carried in the air dissolve in the mucus they are detected by the cilia. The sensors send a signal to the brain, and you experience a smell.

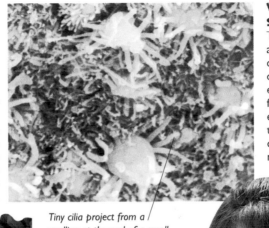

Tiny cilia project from a swelling at the end of a smell sensor in the nasal lining.

NASAL LINING

The nasal cavity is lined with millions of tiny hairlike cilia. Cilia move rhythmically to carry dirt and bacteria they have trapped down to the throat, where they are swallowed.

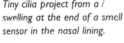

WHAT YOU CAN SMELL

The sense of smell allows us to distinguish over 10,000 different odors. Such sensitivity enables people to tell if food is fresh enough to eat safely or to enjoy the smell of flowers and other scents. It can also make a person aware of odors, such as burning, that may indicate danger.

THE HEART

The heart is divided in two. Each side has two chambers, a smaller upper chamber, the atrium, and a larger lower chamber, the ventricle. Blood enters the heart through the atria, and leaves from the ventricles.

Right atrium

Right ventricle

THE VITAL PUMP

The heart is a muscular pump that beats about 70 times a minute – over two billion times in a lifetime – to propel blood around your body. With each heartbeat, the heart relaxes and fills with blood from the veins, and then contracts to squeeze blood out along your arteries. When the body needs more oxygen, the heart automatically speeds up.

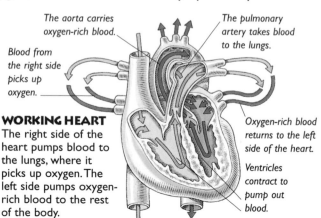

The aorta carries oxygen-rich blood.

The pulmonary artery takes blood to the lungs.

Blood from the right side picks up oxygen.

Oxygen-rich blood returns to the left side of the heart.

WORKING HEART
The right side of the heart pumps blood to the lungs, where it picks up oxygen. The left side pumps oxygen-rich blood to the rest of the body.

Ventricles contract to pump out blood.

BLOOD SUPPLY

Blood carries oxygen to your body through a system of tubes (blood vessels). The heart also needs oxygen all the time but it cannot get it from the blood it pumps. Instead it has its own supply in blood vessels that surround the heart like a net.

The muscular heart wall is supplied with oxygen through its own system of blood vessels.

HEART STRINGS

Heart strings anchor the valve between the atrium and the ventricle in place and stop the valve from turning inside out, like an umbrella blown the wrong way. The valve prevents blood from flowing backward when the heart contracts.

Heart strings are attached to the heart wall and the valve.

Valve

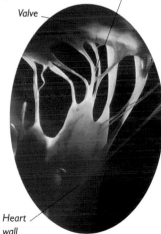

HEART VALVES

Valves guard the exits from the heart. When the ventricles contract, the three flaps of the valve open as blood is pumped out. When the ventricles relax, the three flaps close, to stop blood flowing back into the ventricle.

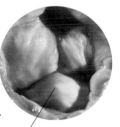

Closed valve prevents blood rom flowing backward.

Open valve allows blood to flow out of the heart.

Heart wall

BLOOD VESSELS

Blood vessels are tubes that carry blood around the body. Stretched out, the blood vessels would extend over 62,500 miles (100,000 km). The largest blood vessels are the arteries, that carry blood away from the heart, and the veins, that return blood to the heart. Linking the two are microscopic tubes called capillaries – these carry blood through the body tissues to all the cells.

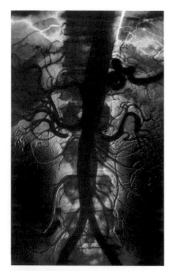

BLOOD ROUTE
An angiogram of the abdomen shows the main arteries. The large artery is the aorta, the main artery from the heart. Branching out from it are the arteries that supply the stomach, liver, and kidneys. At the base of the aorta two arteries fork down to the legs.

ARTERIES AND VEINS
Arteries have thick, strong walls to stand up to the high pressure of blood produced when the heart beats. Veins have thinner walls because in them blood pressure is lower as blood returns to the heart.

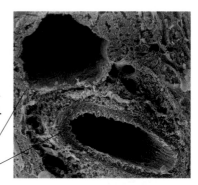

Veins have thin vessel walls.

The vessel walls of an artery are thick.

ARTERY WALL

A magnified view of a slice through an artery shows its thick, elastic wall. When the heart contracts it sends a surge of blood along the artery. If the artery is near the body's surface this surge can be felt as a pulse.

Capillaries are only just wider than the blood cells that pass down them.

FINE TUBING

Capillaries have thin walls; food and oxygen can pass through them to supply tissue cells. Wastes move in the opposite direction.

BLOOD NETWORK

This model of an arm shows its bones and some of the blood vessels that supply it. Like other parts of the body, the arm and hand receive oxygen-rich blood pumped from the heart along arteries (red). Blood that has supplied oxygen to tissues in the arm and hand returns to the heart along veins (blue).

Inside the artery wall are elastic muscle fibers that allow it to expand and shrink when blood surges along it.

Vein

Artery

RIVER OF LIFE

As blood flows past the body cells it supplies them with everything they need to stay alive. It also helps defend your body against disease. Blood is made of billions of tiny blood cells floating in a watery liquid called plasma. Plasma transports food around the body and removes waste. Red blood cells carry life-giving oxygen. White blood cells fight infection by destroying germs.

This tiny branch of an artery measures no more than 0.002 inch (0.025 mm) across. It is full of red blood cells.

A LONG WAY TO GO
During its life of about 120 days, a red blood cell travels an amazing 9.3 miles (15 km) each day along blood vessels.

This white blood cell is a T-lymphocyte, which is covered in tiny feelers that help it find bacteria to destroy.

ON GUARD
White blood cells help defend the body against disease. One type of white cell, called a T-lymphocyte, attacks and destroys invading bacteria and other germs. Another type, called B-lymphocytes, release germ-killing chemicals called antibodies.

DROP OF BLOOD

Billions of red blood cells are needed to transport oxygen from your lungs. A red cell's dimpled, doughnut-like shape provides a large surface for absorbing oxygen in the lungs.

Red blood cells greatly outnumber spiky white blood cells in this drop of blood.

White blood cell

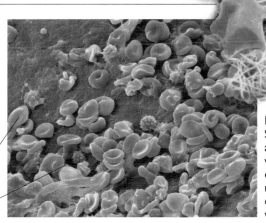

GERM-EATERS

Neutrophils and macrophages are white blood cells that hunt down bacteria and other germs and eat them. These germ-eaters are carried by the blood to wherever germs have invaded. There they pass through the walls of tiny blood vessels called capillaries into the tissues, where they track down the invaders.

NETWORK

Strands of fibrin appear in the blood when a blood vessel is damaged. They form a net that traps red blood cells. These form a clot which seals the hole.

A neutrophil squeezes through the wall of a capillary into the surrounding tissues.

Platelets plug small leaks in blood vessels and make the blood produce fibrin nets.

BODY DEFENSES

Every second of every day, the body is under threat from bacteria, viruses, and other germs that cause infections and diseases. The body uses various strategies to defend itself from this attack. Roaming phagocytes eat any germs that they detect. The immune system targets specific germs with chemicals called antibodies and "remembers" each invader so it can quickly respond if they enter the body again.

Strands of bacteria (white) crowd together on the surface of this tongue. Bacteria and other germs enter the body through the mouth.

SURFACE DEFENSES

The skin and the lining of your nose, mouth, and other body openings form a barrier that germs cannot easily cross. The tonsils in the throat deal with bacteria in the mouth and tears wash away dirt and bacteria from the surface of the eyes.

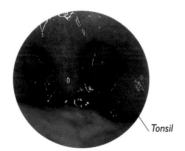

Tonsil

Tonsils are packed with white blood cells that destroy germs.

Tears contain a special chemical that kills bacteria.

DESTROYERS

Phagocytes are white blood cells that destroy germs by eating them. Projections on the surface of the phagocyte surround the germ and pull it inside the cell, where it is digested.

Malaria parasite inside a red blood cell.

WHITE DEFENDERS

Neutrophils are the commonest type of white blood cell. When germs enter the body, neutrophils are often first on the scene. They leave the blood, move into the affected tissues, and destroy the germs.

Attracted by bacterial chemicals, a phagocyte moves forward to engulf and destroy the mass of smaller rod-shaped bacteria.

MALARIA

The body finds it difficult to defend itself against certain diseases. Malaria is caused by a tiny parasite injected into the blood by biting mosquitoes. The parasites invade red blood cells, which then burst. This makes the person very ill and feverish. Treatment by specific drugs is the only cure.

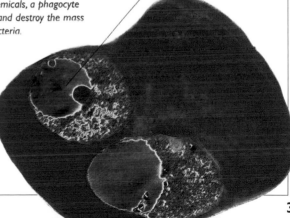

LUNGS

The body needs a constant supply of oxygen to release energy from food in order to stay alive. Every time you breathe, you take fresh air into your lungs and breathe out stale air. The lungs absorb oxygen from the fresh air, and this is taken into the bloodstream. At the same time, carbon dioxide waste from the body is carried to the lungs by the bloodstream and breathed out.

Vocal cords open

Vocal cords closed

VOCAL CORDS

During normal breathing the vocal cords are open. They close up when a person speaks, and air passing between them makes them vibrate and produce sounds, which are shaped in the mouth into speech.

PROTECTIVE CAGE

The two lungs are on either side of the heart. The lungs are surrounded by a protective bony "cage" made of 12 pairs of ribs. The rib cage moves up and down to draw air in and expel it out of your lungs.

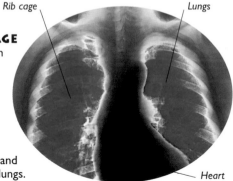

Rib cage

Lungs

Heart

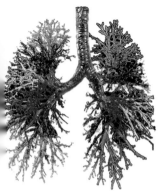

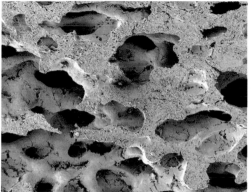

OXYGEN UPTAKE

Millions of tiny air sacs, or alveoli, are found bunched together at the ends of bronchioles. They provide a huge surface for absorbing oxygen rapidly into the bloodstream.

BRONCHIAL TREE

Each of the lungs is a branching network of airways that resembles an upside-down tree. The "trunk" of this bronchial tree is the windpipe; its branches are called bronchi and bronchioles.

AIR CLEANERS

Masses of miniscule hairlike cilia line your windpipe and bronchi. The cilia beat rhythmically to move dust and germs up to your throat and away from your delicate lungs, where they would cause damage.

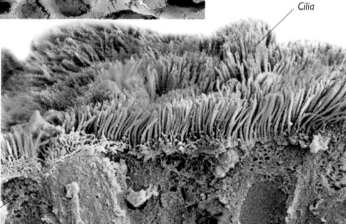

Cilia

Windpipe

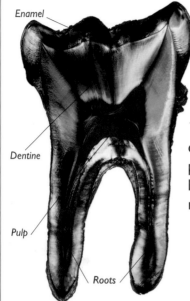

Enamel

Dentine

Pulp

Roots

CHOPPING TEETH

Food is eaten to give the body energy and the materials it needs for growth. Before food can be swallowed, it is chopped up by the teeth. There are four types of teeth. Chisel-like incisors cut food, pointed canines grip it, flat-topped premolars and large molars grind it. Young children have 20 milk teeth. In late childhood these are replaced by 32 permanent teeth.

INSIDE A TOOTH

A tooth is covered by hard enamel on the upper part, the crown. Bonelike dentine forms most of the inside of the tooth and extends into the roots. In the center the soft pulp contains blood vessels and nerves.

Second layer of teeth in jawbone above milk teeth

EMERGING TEETH

Children have two sets of teeth in their mouth. The first set, the milk teeth, will be replaced by a set of permanent teeth that are "waiting" to emerge from the gums.

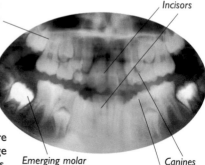

Incisors

Canines

Emerging molar

Tooth enamel

ENAMEL RIDGES

Under a microscope, white tooth enamel looks ridged because it is made up of rods of calcium salts. This structure makes enamel the hardest substance in the body, able to resist the wear and tear caused by chewing.

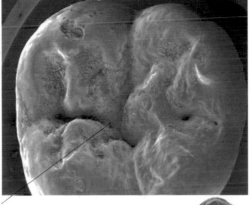

BUMPY TEETH

Molar teeth have a broad surface with four raised edges called cusps. As two molar teeth come together to chew, food is ground and crushed between their cusps.

Sticky plaque, a mixture of food and bacteria, may build up if teeth are not cleaned. The bacteria release acids that damage enamel and cause tooth decay.

Close up view of dentine

DENTINE INSIDE THE TOOTH

Bonelike dentine has a network of minute channels. Fine tubes pass through the channels and connect the soft pulp to the nerve endings.

DIGESTION

The food we eat is too complex for the body to use. First it must be digested, or broken down, to make it easy to absorb. This happens in the digestive system using chemical digesters, called enzymes. As food is swallowed it passes down a tube called the esophagus to the stomach. Here it is partly digested and passed into the small intestine, where digestion is completed. Waste is expelled as feces.

The lining of the esophagus under a microscope.

SLIPPERY LINING

The lining of the esophagus is covered with tiny folds. These folds trap slimy mucus, making it easier for food to slide down the esophagus from the throat into the stomach.

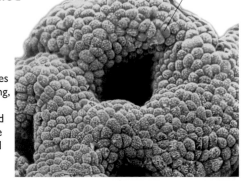

Stomach lining

STOMACH LINING

Glands in deep holes in the stomach lining, called gastric pits, produce strong acid and enzymes. These start to digest food as it is churned up by the stomach.

SMALL INTESTINE

Millions of tiny fingerlike villi cover the inside of the small intestine. As liquid food swirls around the villi it is broken into simple food molecules and digestion is completed. The villi rapidly absorb digested food through all parts of their surface.

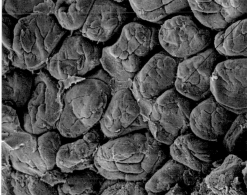

Tightly packed villi, each no longer than 0.04 in (1 mm)

COLON

The 5 ft (1.5 m) long colon is the main part of the large intestine. The colon starts near your appendix and winds up, across, and down your abdomen before it reaches your waste-expelling rectum.

The flat lining of the large intestine *The lining of the small intestine*

MEETING POINT

Where the small and large intestines meet there is a change. The lining of the small intestine is folded so it can absorb digested food. The lining of the large intestine is flatter, with openings to glands that release slimy mucus. This helps to slide dry feces along it easily.

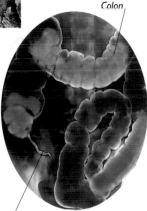

Colon

Appendix

CHEMICAL FACTORY

The liver adjusts and maintains the correct chemical composition of the blood. It has two blood supplies: one from the heart, and one from the digestive system. The liver is packed with millions of cells called hepatocytes, which have more than 500 different functions. These include breaking down toxins (poisons) and other chemicals, and processing and storing nutrients absorbed from the small intestine.

HEAT PICTURE

Heat released by the liver keeps the body warm. This thermograph shows the skin temperature of an eight-year-old boy. The hottest parts of his body are white and the coolest purple.

LIVER SCAN

This special X-ray has produced a "slice" of the upper abdomen, to show the large liver and the gall bladder.

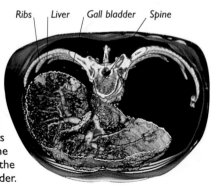

Ribs   Liver   Gall bladder   Spine

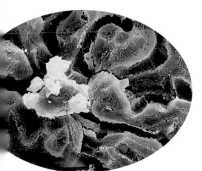

PROCESSING BLOOD

A complex network of blood vessels carries blood throughout the liver. The liver cells (hepatocytes) are bathed in blood so they can carry out their job of processing the blood efficiently.

PROCESSING PLANT

Liver cells are arranged along channels called sinusoids, or blood-filled spaces. As blood flows through the sinusoids the liver cells "process" the blood, by removing nutrients, toxins, micro-organisms, and debris.

This resin cast of the liver's blood vessels shows the network of arteries, veins, capillaries, and sinusoids.

The folded lining of the gall bladder

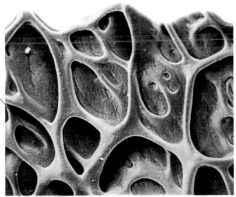

INSIDE A GALL BLADDER

The gall bladder is a small baglike organ that sits beneath your liver. It stores bile, a greenish-yellow liquid produced by your liver. When food is being digested, the gall bladder squirts bile into the small intestine to help break down fats.

WASTE DISPOSAL

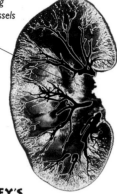

Branching blood vessels inside a kidney

KIDNEY'S BLOOD SUPPLY

This X-ray of a kidney injected with a special dye shows the arteries that supply it with over 1 pint (450 ml) of blood each minute.

Two bean-shaped kidneys are located in the abdomen, just below the stomach. The kidneys "clean" blood by removing poisonous waste that has been produced by the body's cells and excess water. Inside each kidney there are a million microscopic filtering units called nephrons. Waste and water from the blood passes into the nephrons and is turned into urine. "Clean" blood then leaves the kidney. Urine flows to the bladder, from where it is released.

A podocyte surrounds a blood capillary.

PODOCYTE

Podocytes are special cells with "tendrils." They wrap themselves around minute blood vessels or capillaries to form a ball, called a glomerulus. Water and waste are "sieved" out of the blood in the glomerulus.

FILTERING UNIT

A cluster of blood capillaries called a glomerulus is surrounded by a cup-shaped capsule. Water and waste pass from the capillaries into the capsule and the long, winding tube attached to it.

Glomerulus removed from its cup.

FROM KIDNEY TO BLADDER

The kidneys are found in the abdomen. Urine made in the kidneys passes down thin tubes called ureters and is stored in the bladder until it can be released.

This hollow part of the kidney funnels urine into the ureters.

The bladder stores urine.

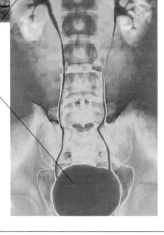

CONNECTED BALLS

The arteries that supply blood to the kidneys lead to these tiny balls called glomeruli. Blood pressure inside each glomerulus forces water and waste out through the capillary walls.

EGG AND SPERM

A developing egg in a follicle

Adult humans, like other living things, can produce young. Humans reproduce when a male sex cell, a sperm, joins with a female sex cell, an egg. A woman usually releases a single egg each month from one of her two ovaries. A man produces millions of sperm every day in his two testes. When a man and a woman have sexual intercourse, sperm are released inside the woman. The sperm swim toward her fallopian tubes in search of an egg.

GROWING EGG

At birth, a girl's ovaries already contain millions of immature eggs, each in a tiny sac called a follicle. After puberty, one egg develops each month. Its follicle expands and follicle cells nourish the growing egg until it is released.

EGG CARRIER

The narrow oviduct, called the fallopian tube, carries newly released eggs from an ovary to the uterus. Lining the fallopian tube are tiny, hairlike cilia. These cilia beat rhythmically to waft the egg toward the uterus.

Cilia move an egg along a fallopian tube. An egg cannot move by itself.

Head

Tail

SPEEDY SWIMMERS
Sperm have a very streamlined shape. This enables them to swim easily through liquids. A sperm's long tail thrashes fast to push its flattened head forward on its route toward the egg.

ENERGY SUPPLY
A sperm's head, which carries genetic information, is linked to its long tail by a neck. The neck contains tiny powerhouses, called mitochondria, that provide energy for movement.

Newly-made sperm are visible inside a cut-open tubule.

SPERM FACTORY
Sperm are made by tiny tightly coiled tubes, called seminiferous tubules, are packed into a man's testes. Lining each tubule are cells that produce the sperm and nourish them. Hundreds of millions of sperm are made each day. They take two months to mature and start moving.

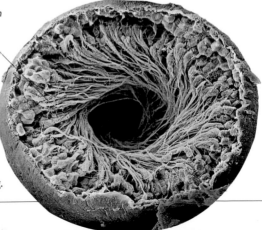

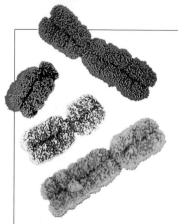

NEW LIFE

When a sperm meets an egg, following sexual intercourse, they join together in a process called fertilization. As the fertilized egg travels toward the uterus, it divides to form an embryo. The embryo attaches itself to the lining of the uterus. After eight weeks of growth it is called a fetus. Nine months after fertilization the fetus is fully developed and ready to be born.

CHROMOSOMES
Chromosomes are found in the nucleus of every cell in your body. They contain about 100,000 instructions, called genes, that are needed to make a human being.

FERTILIZATION
When sperm meet an egg they swim around it, releasing chemicals to penetrate its outer barrier. Eventually one sperm manages to penetrate the egg and its nucleus fuses with that of the egg. Fertilization has taken place.

A single sperm breaks through the surface of the egg to fertilize it.

BALL OF CELLS
Three days after fertilization, and still traveling toward the uterus, the tiny embryo consists of a berrylike ball of 16 cells.

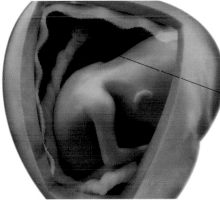

UNBORN CHILD
This model shows a five-month-old fetus in the uterus. Its head, back, and tiny arms are easy to see.

Blood containing food and oxygen travels along this umbilical cord to the fetus from its mother.

AMNIOTIC FLUID
A fetus floats in a watery liquid, called amniotic fluid, inside the uterus. The fluid protects it from shocks and jolts.

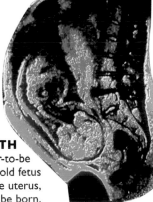

READY FOR BIRTH
A side view of a mother-to-be shows her nine-month-old fetus upside down in the uterus, ready to be born.

INDEX

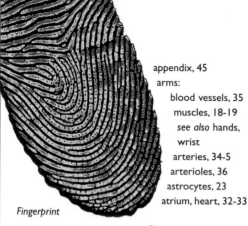

Fingerprint

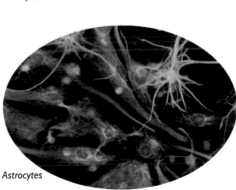

Astrocytes

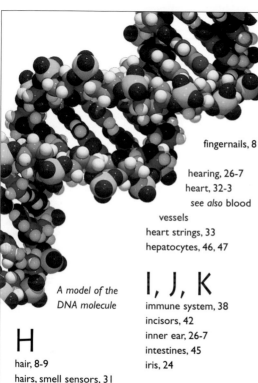

A model of the DNA molecule

H

hair, 8-9
hairs, smell sensors, 31
hands:
    bones, 13, 16

fingernails, 8

hearing, 26-7
heart, 32-3
    see also blood
vessels
heart strings, 33
hepatocytes, 46, 47

I, J, K

immune system, 38
incisors, 42
inner ear, 26-7
intestines, 45
iris, 24

joints, 12-13
    see also bones,

muscles
keratin, 8, 9
kidneys, 48-9
knees, bones, 17

L

large intestine, 45
larynx, 40
legs, fractures, 17
lens, eyes, 24
liver, 46-7
    cells, 5, 47
lungs, 40-1
    see also alveoli
lymphocytes, 36

M

macrophages, 37
malaria, 39
melanin, 7
milk teeth, 42
mitochondria, 51
molars, 42, 43
motor neurons, 22

mouth:
    taste, 28-9
    teeth, 42-3
    tongue, 28-9
    tonsils, 38
mucus, 44, 45
muscles, 18-19
myofibrils, 19
myopia, 24

N

nails, 8
nasal cavity, 30-1
nephrons, 48, 49
nerves, 22-3
nervous system, 20-31
    hearing, 26-7
    neurons and nerves,
    22-3
    seeing, 24-5
    smell, 30-1
    taste, 28-9
    see also brain
neuroglia, 23
neurons, 20, 22-3

Seminiferous tubules

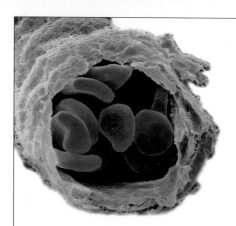

Red cells in arteriole